I'm In My Feelings Series

OTHER BOOKS BY ROBERT M. DRAKE

Spaceship (2012)
The Great Artist (2012)
Science (2013)
Beautiful Chaos (2014)
Beautiful Chaos 2 (2014)
Black Butterfly (2015)
A Brilliant Madness (2015)
Beautiful and Damned (2016)
Broken Flowers (2016)
Gravity: A Novel (2017)
Star Theory (2017)
Chaos Theory (2017)
Light Theory (2017)
Moon Theory (2017)
Dead Pop Art (2017)
Chasing The Gloom: A Novel (2017)
Moon Matrix (2018)
Seeds of Wrath (2018)
Dawn of Mayhem (2018)
The King is Dead (2018)
What I Feel When I Don't Want To Feel (2019)
What I Say To Myself When I Need To Calm The
Fuck Down (2019)
What I Say When I'm Not Saying A Damn Thing
(2019)
What I Mean When I Say Miss You, Love You &
Fuck You (2019)

For Excerpts and Updates please follow:

Instagram.com/rmdrk
Facebook.com/rmdrk
Twitter.com/rmdrk

ISBN: 978-1-7326900-8-0

Book Cover: Robert M. Drake

For The Ones Who Feel Trapped

CONTENTS

What I Say To Myself When I Need To Calm The Fuck Down

ROBERT M. DRAKE

IF YOU

If you haven't
been yourself lately.

If you've ever
felt lost

or empty

and

cannot explain why.

If you've been looking
for something

you don't even know
exists.

If you've been asking questions,
perhaps even

the wrong ones,
and still

have yet
to receive an answer.

If you don't know

who you are.

If you don't know
why you're here.

If you don't know
why you feel

the way you feel.

And lastly,
if you feel more alone

than the night before.

I understand you.

I feel what you feel.

I've asked the same questions
and I've wondered

all my life
about
the same things,
too.

I have my own demons
and I'm still struggling

with them

every day.

This is my truth.

This is my soul...
and I hope

my horrors leave you
with something.

I hope
they give you

the strength you
need to carry on.

The courage you need
to move on,

to let go
of whatever hurts you.

There still hope...
there always is,

no matter how far
in you are.

The light,
that little spark

of hope,

will always
show you the way.

SOME PEOPLE

Some people
never give up

on the people
they love.

And some will call it
a curse—a burden

of pain
and suffering,

but I call it

struggling
and fighting

for someone worth it—for
something you know

you deserve.

DO NOT LET…

Don't let your heart
lose hope.

The wrong people
will exit your life

when they have to
and the right ones

will find you
when you need them most.

Trust the process.

Find comfort
in your timing

and let time decide
who gets to stay.

Worry less
and trust the process

a little more.

OF YOURSELF

You have to take care
of yourself entirely.

Not just your heart
but your mind,

soul and body.

You have to protect
yourself at all costs

but not just from relationships
and getting your heart broken

but from external factors
that are meant to bring you down.

Protect your mind
and your thoughts.

Protect your body
from processed foods.

Protect your soul
from bad energies

and focus
on what matters

to you.

Focus
on what you love.

Focus
on spreading love.

Focus on healing.

So many of us
are wanting to heal.

And so many of us
don't know how

or where to start.

Just focus on yourself.
Take time on yourself.

It all begins
with you.

That's all.

LEARN THIS

You have to learn
how to accept yourself

for who you are.

Be comfortable
in your own skin,
you know?

You have to embrace it,
make the best of it.

And if you're not happy,
then you have the right

to take time
on yourself,

to work on yourself.

But you have to be patient.

It's not going to happen
overnight

and it's not
something

someone else
could do for you either.

You are what you are
and what you want

to change
is something

only you can do
for yourself.

Just remember
to stay beautiful, baby,

and remember
to always chase

the things
you deserve..

CONVERSATIONS

*Sometimes
having a conversation*

*in a parked car
for hours*

*can heal you
in ways you never thought
possible.*

It can be therapeutic.

*It can sometimes save you
from yourself.*

AFRAID OF US

They want us
to be ourselves

but only
if it's within their terms.

They want us
to be free

but as long
as we don't go
far enough.

And then
they ask us

why are we so mad.

They ask us
why are we so bitter

towards the future
and so hateful

towards the past.

So much
that they become

afraid of us
in the present.

So much
that they use the media

to dumb us down—to
calm us down.

To lie to us
and hide the truth.

The problem isn't us.
The problem is them...

the older generation
who closed our future.

The older generation
who wanted peace

but failed to grant it
with love.

No.

Instead they brought war.

They brought death
and blood
and pain

and suffering
to the future generations.

Then they wonder
why we are so *goddamn mad.*

You killed everything
we stand for.

Everything that's beautiful.

Everything that gives light
and life

and it all was done
to make money.

Something you also
created

to oppress us.

Something you created
to manufacture

this fake happiness
we have

for yourselves.

DO NOT RUN

You shouldn't run back
to those who broke you.

To those
who've left you

in the dark.

You can't grow a flower
without the use of light.

Sometimes
You have to grow a garden
in the middle of a desert.

Let that sink in.

You beautiful, motherfucker.

A LITTLE PAIN

You don't realize
how much you deserve,

not until
you've been through hell

with someone.

The same way
you don't appreciate love

without going
through a little

pain.

I CARE

And you pretend
you don't care.

And you act
like it doesn't bother you.

And you want to forget
but all you do is remember.

And it hurts even more
when you're alone.

And everyone is laughing
but deep down inside you're sad.

And you try to move on
but can't.

And you want to let go
but some things

are just too damn hard
to get rid of.

And you cry
when no one is around.

And you want to be happy

but you find it difficult
to laugh again.

And you try so hard
to fill the void with other people.

And sometimes those same people
make you feel more alone.

And you're lost
without the one you left behind.

And you just want to be found.
(Anywhere but here)

And you just want
to put everything behind you.

And you've tried almost everything
and nothing has worked.

And this is how you live your life.

This is how it hurts.

This is how the stars die,
but also,

how they are born.

This is how you take it all in.

The pain fills
and the sorrow follows

and the memories can't seem
to fade.

It hurts… as it always does
and as it should.

Sometimes you just can't
get it together

without the people
you love.

EMPTY AND POWERLESS

You tell people
how badly I hurt you—how

quick I was
to leave you.

You play victim
and make it seem

like I was some kind
of terrible person.

You say this
and you say that

but what you fail to say is

how selfish you were.

How isolated
you made me feel.

And how hard it was
to get through to you.

You made me feel
less human.

You made me feel
empty and powerless.

AndI don't
need that in my life.

So please,
don't spread rumors

and lies
because I didn't see

eye to eye with you.

And don't be mad
because I didn't stay.

Be mad
because you failed to give me

what I needed
and you failed

to give yourself
what you deserved.

WAKING UP

That's the thing.

Some people are finally
realizing their worth.

They are finally understanding
what they deserve

and what they don't.

They're making better choices
and giving themselves

sunlight
when they need it most.

And it's a beautiful thing
to witness.

Amen.

HELL IS HELL

People who've been
through hell

only want attention
and love.

They want peace
and honesty.

They want something real
and something worth

their time.

That's all.

THEMSELVES

I never understood this...

how some people
will live these happy lives

with people
they say they love

and still
find it in them

to cheat—still
find it in them

to go home
and act like

everything is okay.

I never understood this...
they can't find it

in them
to leave people behind

but find it in them
to live these double lives

with double meanings
and hurt everyone

involved
including

themselves.

YOUR VOICE

You don't have to
raise your voice

to get your point
across.

Let your truth
flow without violence.

Let your truth
flow with love

and kindness.

And know
how many will hear you

but only a few
will understand

what's in your heart.

So pay attention,
speak your truth

the best way
you know how,

and keep the ones
who are willing to listen

close.

That alone
will make the difference

between life
and death.

FALLS APART

I don't want you
to tell me

how I should feel.

I want you
to hold me

while I'm breaking down
and just be there

for me,
quietly,

until everything we know
falls apart.

TRUTH HURTS

You have to
own up

to what you do
and live

with the consequences

even if the truth
hurts.

THINGS WORK

I gave you my heart
and although

you broke it,
I still believe

that you have
some goodness left

inside of you.

I still believe
that you have a good heart.

Maybe we were just
at the wrong place

and at the wrong time.

Or maybe
I just pushed you

too far out.

I'm sorry for everything
I've caused.

I just wish

I could take it all back
and relive

what we had
and make things work.

A FLOWER

A flower grew
inside of me

and now
I worry about you
leaving it.

I worry
about everything you've given it

and how empty
my life would be

if you suddenly
took it away.

MY LIFE

My life isn't perfect
and I understand

how it's not
meant to be.

I drown,
I fall,

and sometimes
I want to die,

but that doesn't
make me give up.

I'm still here.

Fighting.

Pushing back
and doing so

the best way I can.

Life is hard,
it wants to kill me,

but it doesn't stop me.

It only gives me
more strength,

more breath,
and above all,

a little more

love
for life.

IT HURTS

It hurts
and sometimes

it feels
like I'm breaking into

a million different piece's

I didn't know
existed.

FROM THE START

I'm praying for you
because

I just want to see you
healthy again.

I want to see you
smiling

and laughing
again…

because I miss
who you were.

I miss
the person you

used to be
before the darkness

took over
your body.

It's sad to say,
but I want

my old friend back.

I want the person
I grew up with

and not the person
I barely know.

If only it were
this simple...

I would go back
in time

and save you. I'll

take away
everything that ever hurt you

from the start.

TURNS OUT

Turns out,

some of the best
advice I've ever received

was
that of my own.

*"To let go
when there was nothing*

*left to hold on to
and to forgive*

*when it was
the last thing*

*I could have
done."*

NOTHING TO SAY

No matter
what you're going through,

having someone
to listen to you

helps...

even if
they have

nothing to say.

AND LOVE

Love
and love

and love.

Time is too short
to spend it

doing anything else.

AMEN.

ALONE

You hurt
when you're alone,

of course
you do.

The best kind
of people

always feel
the rain

a little harder.

ALONE 2

You want
what kills you,

of course you do.

You want to
feel love

at its fullest potential,
even if

it's the last thing
you feel.

THAT IS LOVE

It's okay
to be alone

but not to
feel alone.

Everyone needs
someone to go home to.

Someone to claim
them as their own.

That's love.

THE PROBLEM

That's the problem.

You hold on
when you should be

letting go
and you stand still

when you should be
moving on.

IT IS NOT

Giving someone time
is a very scary thing

because

you don't know
if they'll come back

to you
or forget you.

You don't know
if it will help

the relationship
or make it worse.

Time

is a very
tricky thing

and sometimes
it's on your side

while other times
it's not.

SOLEY ON YOU

And how it hurts
depends solely

on how much
you loved.

And

how you let go
depends solely

on how many times
you've fallen,

but also,

how many times
you've learned

to move on.

That's all.

WHERE TO GO

I know nothing
and everything

at the same time.

The same way
I need to let go

and to move on
but don't have

anywhere
to go.

SAD PEOPLE

The saddest people
hurt differently.

They smile
when they cry.

They always look happy
and they have a hard time

explaining
what they feel.

WOLVES

Some people
are wolves

in sheep's clothing.

They give you
a little kindness

and expect you
to give them

your heart—
your soul.

Be careful.

Never fall in love
with someone

because
they've shown you

a little attention
and

never give them
your heart

until you feel

like they have given
you theirs.

WHAT KILLS ME

It's that little bit
of hope

that kills me.

That slight chance
that maybe

you and I
could work

things out.

That little light
that keeps flickering

in the back of my head,

the one that keeps
reminding me

not

to give up on you.

BLESSINGS

It hurts,
of course it does,

because

you keep making excuses
for them.

You keep
giving them chances

when you know
you should be

moving on—when
you know

you deserve better.

And that's the problem.

You care
and you do

so unconditionally.

No matter
how many reasons

they give you
not to.

You care
and sometimes

that's more a curse
than a blessing.

NO TIME

It's not
that I don't have time

for you.

It's just...
I finally know

what I deserve.

SOMETHING YOU LOVE

You have a life
and you have

to live it.

You have
to do

whatever it is
that makes you

feel good.

Whatever it is
that makes

you happy,
but really happy.

And not
just for a moment,

but for as long
as you can.

You have to do
what brings you peace,
just do it.

And there will be
consequences.

Sometimes good,
sometimes bad,

but if it makes you
happy,

then do it.

If it feels like home,
then follow it.

Don't doubt yourself.

Don't fall
into the flaws.

And don't listen
to the outside world

when they
tell you otherwise.

If it makes you feel good,
then do it

and don't stop.

Don't look back

and don't ask
too many questions.

You have a life
and you have to live it,

so you might as well
live it

doing something
you love.

TELL ME

Tell me
why your heart

is exhausted.

Why it keeps
running circles,

staying
in the same place

when you know
it doesn't

belong.

ADVENTURE

It's never too late
to start over.

Never too late
to be

who you want
to be—to let go

of whatever

past
that is holding

you down.

And above all,
it's never too late

to find love—to
feel young again

and to seek

whatever
adventure

that awaits.

IT IS SAD

It's sad

because
you're still grieving
the people

you've lost.

The ones
who've moved on

and the ones
you can't

get out
of your heart.

REMEMBER

You have to
live

as if
it's the last thing

you were meant
to do

and love hard
as if

it's the last way
you want

to be
remembered.

SHOW ME

Show me a person
who has loved.

A person
who has fought

for the people
they need.

And I'll give you
a lifetime

full of brokenness
and a heart

full of sadness

too beautiful
to bear.

EVERY CHANCE

What you share
with other people

is special.

Whether it be
a simple conversation

or days together
or apart.

What you share
with them

is beautiful
and should be

protcctcd
no matter what.

You never know
when it's the last time

you'll see someone
you love

and they'll never know
how much

they mean to you,

not unless
you tell them

every chance
you get.

NO JUDGEMENT

No more walls.
No more limitations.

No more labeling
and discrimination.

I want to be free
of judgment

and I want
to love

who I want to love
and have it

no other way
than that

of my own.

MISTAKES

You can't mistake
vulnerability

for weakness.

Some people
are forged

from breaking apart.

They become stronger
the moment

they let go.

The moment
they pour themselves

to those
they love

and do
whatever it takes

to make things work.

They risk their lives
for the people they need...

and to be honest,

there's nothing weak
about that.

YEARS AND YEARS

It took me years
to understand

that you can't save
everyone.

That you
can only be there
for them,

care for them,
and love them

unconditionally.

Even if that means
letting them go.

HOW IT HAPPENS

That's how it happens.

First you feel,
then you love.

You fall.
You break.

You learn.

Then you accept,
move on,

and start over.

It's sad isn't it?

To think
how many times

you'll go through this
and how many times

you'll fall in love
and go through pain...

without fully
understanding

what it is

you really deserve.

BOTH DARK AND LIGHT

We have both
darkness and light

in our souls.

Love and hate.
Happiness and sadness.

So to say the least,
you choose

what to let out.

You choose
what you let in.

In other words,
it's completely

up to you
how to let things
affect you.

So… sometimes

a bad thing
can be a good thing
and a good thing

can be a bad thing.

The power
is in your perspective.

In your ability
to look past the margins.

To look past
the social commentaries,

that is,
the way

we're expected
to react.

And remember,
karma is a bitch,

and what you put out
usually tends

to come around
again.

So maybe not today
or tomorrow,

but one day.

Therefore,
you should try,

with every fiber
in your being,

to be kind.

You never know
what kind of blessing

is heading your way.

And you never know
whose life

you'll be changing
with the passing

of time.

DRAWN BY PEOPLE

We are attracted
to people

who are like us—who
relate to us.

So if all you do
is break me

and hurt me,
then perhaps,

in some sense,

that says
more about me

than it says
about you.

That's all.

HAUNTED

We're always haunted
by the past

and the future.

By what has caused us
great pain

and this strange idea
of the unknown.

We want success
and not failure.

We want wisdom
and experience

but without
the headaches they bring.

We want balance
and peace

but almost always,
the bright future

is reminded
by the bitter past.

Sadly,
we get nothing good

without some kind
of hurting.

Sadly,
we do not grow

without

a little pain.

EXPLAIN WHY

Of course,
it's easier to pretend
to be happy

than

to reveal
that you're sad.

The world
is sometimes

made of lies
and sometimes

those same lies
bring us both

peace and chaos,
and sadly,

sometimes
no one has enough

courage
to explain why.

THROUGH PAIN

We go through pain…
of course

that's how it happens.

When we have
no one left

to love,

we begin
to love ourselves.

When we have gone
through enough,

we finally realize
what we deserve.

Everyone
has their breaking point.

Everyone
has their point

of no return.

And once you've crossed

that line,
you begin to realize

what you deserve

but what you deserve
will never reveal itself

without going
through the fire—a

little struggle.

Nothing ever comes easy.

Nothing beautiful
is ever revealed

without some kind
of pain.

Remember that.

From generation
to generation,

we are all challenged
and presented

with pain.

And from generation
to generation,

we rise above it.

We learn from experience
and move on.

We pick ourselves up
and learn

to walk again.

Remember that,
too.

DEPENDS

And everything
you feel

depends solely
on how much

you love.

LITTLE MEMORY

There is a little
memory and pain

in everything.

You just have to
pay attention

a little harder
and when you do,

you realize
how much

you're not alone.

THAT IS ALL

I know
what you mean

when you say
you can't handle people

but you have to
have patience

with them.

Because

there are still
some good people

in this world.

All you have to do
is be patient

with them.

That's all.

FORCED TO LEAVE

You don't know
who you are

until

someone you love
leaves you

and you don't know
what you're made of

until

you're forced
to leave

someone you love.

MEET AGAIN

I haven't seen you
in sometime

and I just want to say

how

they say
time heals everything.

How they say
being apart

will help me heal.

It's been four years
since

I last spoke to you
and it's hard to say,

but there hasn't been
a day

or a moment
when I don't think

about you.

You cross my mind
in the most random of times

and you are not here
but

you are
in my heart
all the time.

Rest in paradise,
my sweet brother.

I hope
wherever you've gone...

you've found peace
and love

and tranquility.

Until
we mcet again.

THEY SAY...

They say
you get stepped on

when you're polite...

you get taken
for granted

when you're too kind
and you don't get

taken seriously
if you're too nice.

So the thing is,
they trick you

into thinking
that being an asshole

is the only way
you can get

through to people.

The only way
you can get

what you want.

And they say
that being loud

and violent
is the only way

to get people
to listen.

Well,
I say,

those ideas are wrong.

You must be gentle
to move people.

You must be
open minded

and understanding
to get your point

across
and you definitely
have to be patient.

The old ways
have left our hearts

empty and undone.

The old ways
have left our hearts

broken and unresolved.

No one knows
what to do anymore.

No one knows
how to take feelings

under consideration
anymore.

So I say
to be kind.

To be good.

To be understanding.

To put yourself
in the shoes of others

and really
try to get

in your feelings
and theirs, too.

Be kind.

That's all it is.

Be sensitive
to others

and their horrors—their
pains and struggles.

Be gentle
and soft

with their hearts.

And the more you do,
the more others

will do the same.

Spread positivity,
love, and hope—become
it...

and soon enough,
people will begin

to change.

The revolution starts
with you.

And
it will always

start
with you.

ONE DAY NOW

One of these days
someone

is going to love you
and remind you

of how
you're not meant

to feel alone.

THE VOID

It's hard to say
but sometimes

I want to be
a different person.

Sometimes
I want to go

somewhere new
and start over.

It's horrible,
I know,

but sometimes
I want to let it all

go—leave it
all behind.

So I could find
myself again.

So I could
find that piece

I've been looking for

to fill my void.

Fill whatever it is
I think…

is empty
within my hurting

soul.

THE PEOPLE OUTSIDE

I ruined me
not you.

If I'm broken
it is because

I let it happen.

I was okay
with letting you in—letting

you love me
even if I knew

it was a bad thing
to do.

I did this
to myself,

so stop apologizing
for what you think

you did to me.

You did nothing.
I fell in love.

I got hurt
and now

I'm learning
how to put myself back

together again,
to move on.

How to forgive
myself

for everything
I've caused… to myself.

I'm learning
how it is…

I control
what happens to me

and it is

I, myself…

who lets
people in.

That's all.

HELP ME FORGET

I could see it
in your eyes.

You're keeping yourself
busy

but at the same time,
you're looking

for an escape.

Something
to ease

what hurts a little.

Something
to help you forget.

A LITTLE MORE

No matter how much
you love someone.

There is always
more room

to love
a little more.

LOVE YOURSELF AGAIN

I want
to see you

love yourself.

I want
to see you

do good,
make the right choices,

you know?

But as far
as I can tell,

I cannot
do these things
for you.

I cannot
force change

upon you
and I cannot

make you love
who you are.

That is something
only you can do

for yourself...

whether you like it
or not.

YOU SAY

You say
she's your favorite.

Well,
of course she is,

because
she's a good woman,

but you say it
and say it

and say it

but words
are words

and actions
are actions

and you haven't
been showing it

to her lately.

And in the simplest
of ways, too.

You fail
on asking her

how she's doing.

You fail
on understanding her

and her thoughts.

You fail
on being there for her,

on expressing yourself,
and getting into

her feelings.

You fail
on making time

for her
when she needs it most.

I know it's hard
for you to see

but this is why
she feels

so goddamn alone

sometimes.

AndI know this
because

she tells me.

Because
she pours herself

and shares her deepest feelings
with me.

We go back
and forth

with what hurts
and somewhere in-between

we understand each other.

Unlike you,
she fills me,

and unlike you,
I take her voice

and what she feels
under consideration.

You empty her, man

and she gives me life,

and some way,
somehow,

the time we spend
easing each other's pain

makes it all clear.

Maybe she's with
the wrong person

or maybe
I'm just another fool

who believes in love.

Who believes
in the chaos of it...

in the birth
and death of things.

And this is how
it happens, at least,

for me.

This is how

I fall in love.

I take in what hurts her.

I make sense of it
and make it my own.

And the more
she spews what haunts her,

the more light
I try to shed.

She's a flower
and sometimes

I feel
like I'm giving her

the oxygen
she needs—the
water she needs.

Maybe we're supposed
to be together.

Maybe this is
the beginning

of something beautiful
or maybe

I'm just too involved
to say good-bye.

I don't know…

but the moment
we part ways,

things begin to hurt.

For Christ sake,
I think I need her

and I'm sorry
to tell you this,

but I know
I'll give her

what she deserves.

ACCEPT YOURSELF

Accepting yourself.
Working on yourself.

Taking time
on yourself.

When was the last time
you had your mind

at ease?

When was the last time
you were stress free?

Or had your heart intact?

Life is hard
and there are too many

external factors
pulling at your head—at

your heart.

So why not
have more control

over something

you can control.

Why not
be more self-accepting.

Self-loving.

Do you really need
the extra stress?

Take time on yourself,
I urge this of you.

Learn to love yourself.

Learn how to be
comfortable with yourself.

Do it.
Live by this.
Drink to this.

Self-love
is a beautiful thing—a
holy thing...

and it is something
only you

can provide
to yourself.

Don't be afraid
in taking

a chance.

Don't be afraid
in loving

who you are.

WALKING AWAY

And sometimes

I wonder

if you've made up
your mind.

If you've found
what you've

been looking for
and if

all the questions
your heart had

were answered...

the moment
you walked away.

THE RETURN

You should never
beg someone

to love you,
to care for you.

Those type of things
should never

be asked for.

Those types of things
are given.

They are earned
and almost always

are they equally
returned.

CONVERSATIONS

A conversation
can fix

so many things.

Sometimes
being open

and vulnerable
can change things—save things.

You have to
understand

that people
are going to

disagree with you.

That people
aren't going to see

eye to eye
with you

sometimes.

But you both

can come
to a mutual agreement.

They'll have
what *they* believe in

and so
would you.

You both
just have to

find a mutual ground
and respect that.

That is what
friendship is all about.

LET GO

We adapt.

We learn
to move on.

We learn
to heal,

to forgive,
and keep going...

no matter
who we're forced

to let go.

THE FOLLOWING

Don't focus
on what people say.

People are going to talk,
that's what they do,

and you, well,
you have to

keep going.

You have to
find a way

to get up
and not let anyone

discourage you
from following your path.

Just follow
your heart

no matter what
you see

or hear
at all cost.

HARD TO EXPLAIN

It's hard to explain
what you feel

but here's the thing,
when you find someone

you love
and someone

who loves you back,
you won't

have to explain yourself.

They'll just know.

It's one of those things
you'll share

without

the use of words.

That's love.

DO NOT BE

If it's one thing
I must say,

then
it is this:

It's okay to cry.

It's okay
to feel

like you're not
in control.

It's okay to break,
to not know,

to love
without reason,

and to feel
the same way

you did
last month without any kind
of resolution.

It's okay,

growth takes time
and sometimes

it may take longer
than expected.

It's okay,
feeling lost is normal.

Shedding tears
is beautiful.

Breaking apart
is crucial

and sometimes
loving the wrong person

is meant to happen.

It's okay,
just be patient

with yourself.

Be kind
with yourself

and your feelings.

It's okay,

this is what it takes
to grow.

This is what it takes
to make it through

the day.

*So don't be
so hard on yourself.*

*The best is yet
to come.*

Always.

SAME TIME

You can't explain love.

Let alone,
what people make you feel.

It's one of those things
that make you

lose and find
yourself

at the very
same time.

DESERVE MORE

We settle
for too little

and that's
our biggest flaw.

To sometimes think
and believe

that we don't
deserve better.

That we don't
deserve more.

SOMEONE FOR YOU

Sometimes
the best way

to heal someone
is to sit with them...

even if
you don't have
the words

to comfort them.

You don't have to
say anything

to show someone
you care.

ROB YOU OF...

Do not let anyone
rob you of your light.

Too many people
are stuck within

their own darkness.

Too many people
looking for a way

out.

Looking for a way

in.

Do not let
anyone

rob you
of your light.

Too many people
lost in the shadows.

Too many people
in search

of something
they have yet

to understand.

Protect your light
with your life.

Protect what you love,
even if that means

death.

Protect anything
that makes you feel

young and alive.

There are far too many
things

that bring us
under.

We have far too little
things

that bring us light.

Let us protect
what we have left.

Protect
what they can't

take away.

Our morals.
Our creativity.
Our respect.
Our imaginations.

Our hopes,
dreams,
and our love.

This is all
we have.

This is all
we need.

Protect it.

It is ultimately
the last bit

of humanity
we still have.

A BLESSING

You have to
take care

of yourself,
but not just your heart,

but your mind
and your body.

It, too,
needs your patience
and care.

It, too,
needs your love

and tenderness.

Pay attention
to yourself.

Give yourself
what you need

to stay healthy.

To cleanse
your mind

and body—to
rid it

of any impurities.

Your heart
is the flower.

Your mind
is the soil

and your body
is the stem.

Everything that makes you-you,
is connected

and everything
you take in…

affects everything
you put out.

From your mood
to what terribly hurts,

you must understand
that your well-being

is important
and looking after

yourself
can be a blessing

in disguise.

BREAKING APART

I need you
to care for me

a little harder
on the day's

I feel
like breaking apart.

WANT TO BE

And I'm praying
for the person

I'll become.

I pray that god
grants me peace,

love,
and healing.

I pray
my brokenness

gets understood.

I pray
my emptiness

gets filled

and I pray
everything that hurts me
sets me free...

because

I haven't been

myself lately

and I hope
the future

is as good
as I want it

to be.

SLIP AWAY

You're gone…
and now

I feel
like I haven't been

myself lately.

Like I've lost
a piece of myself

I never knew
I had.

A part
I never thought

existed.

Λ love
I thought I had…

but slowly watched
slip away.

LONG RUN

Take this with
all soul,

all mind,
and all heart:

some heartbreaks
can save your live.

They can bless you
in the long run.

They can change
your path

for the best
and give you

the strength you need

every time
you let

what hurts
out.

BEGINS

With the right person
everything will feel real.

Everything
will just make sense—connect,
you know?

With the right person,
living

will feel
like breathing.

Like healing
from old wounds.

The right person
will do that to you.

They will give you back
your heart

before it began
to break

and take you back
to the beginning...

before things
began to hurt.

Before things
began to fall

apart.